Cardiff
in old picture postcards

by Chrystal Tilney

European Library ZALTBOMMEL / THE NETHERLANDS

GB ISBN 90 288 3259 9

© 1985 European Library – Zaltbommel/The Netherlands

Second edition, 1996: reprint of the original edition of 1985

INTRODUCTION

Cardiff is a city of contrasts — the largest, most cosmopolitan and least Welsh city in Wales, and yet its capital. Its nineteenth century growth and prosperity were based on the coal trade which drew ships and crews from all over the world to the crowded port. To-day in its quiet dockland swarthy skins and exotic names are most likely to belong to second or third generation Cardiffians, and its claim to cosmopolitanism is based on its university.

Now a centre of administration, education and commerce, Cardiff was once the outlet of industrial valleys with the highest production of coal and iron ore in the world. In the last century this export trade transformed the mediaeval borough huddled under the walls of its Norman castle, a castle built on the ruins of a Roman fort — *Caerdydd,* the camp on the Taff.

From that nucleus of fort and castle, still standing in the heart of the modern city, Cardiff burst from the constriction of its mediaeval walls and spread across the mud-flats and meadows to engulf the ancient villages scattered around it — Roath, Llanishen, Canton, Caerau, Fairwater, and the village-city of Llandaff which provided its cathedral on the site where the Celtic saints had built their first Christian church at the ford of the River Taff.

The hey-day of the picture postcard, both functional and as an art-form, coincided with the peak of Cardiff's commercial growth, and its popularity continued during the years when the coal trade declined and the city turned to more diverse industries. War and redevelopment have destroyed much of old Cardiff, giving a poignancy to many of these views, but any selection of viewcards must be incomplete historically, for the aims of the commercial photographer are different from those of the local historian. From time to time I have selected old photographs to give atmosphere or to fill gaps in the postcard record, while trying to avoid repetition of pictures republished in recent years.

Though my aim has been to convey the atmosphere of life in Cardiff from the 1880's to the 1930's, the dating of many postcards can only be approximate. Printers were not above inserting an interesting horse and carriage to fill an empty street, or blocking out telephone wires and tram lines to give an 'olde worlde' look! Even the evidence of postmarks is not completely reliable because of the slow sale or reprinting of many old views.

Despite these drawbacks, view postcards, especially those which also depict people and transport, convey with great immediacy the atmosphere of life in late Victorian, Edwardian and neo-Georgian times. Sir John Ballinger, Cardiff's first Librarian, wrote in his

Guide to Cardiff in 1908 that *The varied life and activities of Cardiff afford plenty of scope for the photographer. Subjects abound among the docks, basins, and quays... The canal and the wharves should not be overlooked, and street scenes and genre studies are plentiful, particularly in the older parts of the City.* These pictures show how both commercial and private photographers followed his advice.

Cardiff doubled its population in the decade 1870-1880, and grew from the 82,761 recorded in 1881 to 280,700 at the last census in 1981. It is impossible, in a work of this size, to present a complete record of such growth and teeming life. In the end, the selection must be a personal one, but in making it I hope to share my enjoyment of, and affection for, the Borough and City of Cardiff depicted in these pages.

The author wishes to thank the following for their permission to reproduce illustrations, and for their kindness and assistance in the research for this book:

Cardiff City Council and the Chief Executive, H.T. Crippin, for Nos. 2, 4, 6, 30, 38, 43, 46, 48; County of South Glamorgan Libraries and the Reference Librarian, M.E. Ling, for Nos. 133, 135, 138, 140; Miss Rhiannon Davies for No. 9; The Dean of Llandaff for Nos. 61, 119, 126, 127, 128, 130; Mrs. R. Ellis for No. 62; Mrs. Audrey Fidler for No. 134; Mr. and Mrs. B.L. Gardiner; Glamorgan Archive Service and the County Archivist, Mrs. Patricia Moore, for Nos. 71, 78, 97; Mrs. Molly Hopkins for No. 137; Mrs. S. Hustwick for No. 63; Mr. and Mrs. Neville James for No. 117; Lock-Newcrews Hill & Partners for No. 26; Peter Leech for permission to quote from *View Around Cardiff* (1969); J.E. McCann for No. 94 from *Thomas Howell and the School at Llandaff* (Browns of Cowbridge, 1972); National Museum of Wales (Library) and the Assistant Librarian, John Kenyon, and his staff for Nos. 11, 19, 28, 47, 74, 75, 76, 77, 84, 85, 89, 98, 99, 108, 116, 98; National Museum of Wales (Welsh Folk Museum) and the Archivist, Arwel Lloyd Hughes, for Nos. 1, 18, 24, 25, 29, 42, 49, 50, 51, 55, 59, 80, 81, 86, 104, 107, 110, 113, 115, 118, 139 and Dr. Elfyn Scourfield, Keeper, Department of Farming and Crafts, for Nos. 92, 105; Miss Gwen Randell for Nos. 16, 27, 53, 67, 122, 123, 129; Canon J.C. Read for No. 114; South Wales Echo for No. 100; Mrs. G. Snook; Mr. Stark for No. 136; University College, Cardiff and the Archives Officer, Mrs. Susan Bellamy, for Nos. 88, 90, 91; Mrs. J.F. Williams for Nos. 120, 121, 124, 132.

COME TO CARDIFF · CARDIFF CIVIC CENTRE · THE CITY BEAUTIFUL

PHOTO BY AEROFILMS

1. The new Cardiff must indeed have seemed 'The City Beautiful' to those dwelling in the cramped courts and rows of the old town. On visitors it had a dramatic effect. H.V. Morton called Cardiff 'the only beautiful city that has grown out of the Industrial Revolution', and Dewi-Prys Thomas, coming from the industrial north, wondered 'that the city of man could be white'.

2. Apart from a few references in Arthurian romance, little was known of pre-Norman Cardiff until the excavations conducted by the 3rd Marquis of Bute. Workmen preparing to build a raised passage from the Castle grounds to his gardens in Cathays broke through the Eastern bank, undisturbed for centuries. Beneath the mediaeval curtain wall and pre-Norman earthwork they found a strong Roman wall and bank. This photograph, taken by W.J. Collings during the excavations in 1898, clearly shows the stages of fortification.

3. The professional and commercial classes of Cardiff showed a civic pride in these discoveries, which explains the presence of the 1901 Committee of Cardiff Orchestral Society in the somewhat incongruous surroundings of the excavated Roman North Gate. This was rebuilt on the ancient foundations as part of a major reconstruction of the rough square of the Roman encampment (see No. 17).

4. William the Conqueror is said to have 'founded Cardiff' in 1091 on his pilgrimage to St. David's. He probably put up temporary defences within the Roman fort, which was strengthened ten years later by Robert Fitzhamon. A motte and bailey were constructed within the Roman square, and the original timber castle was replaced with a stone shell keep on the orders of Robert the Consul in 1147. This was stormed in 1158 by the Welsh lord Ifor Bach, who carried off William, Earl of Gloucester, his wife and son, despite the strong Norman defences. The wooden drawbridge was first replaced by a stone bridge in 1590, and just before this view was taken by Freke in 1898 the moat had been re-excavated and steps built up the mound.

5. At the close of the thirteenth century, under Gilbert de Clare, the early defences were remodelled. Walls divided the area inside the Roman square into middle, inner and outer wards where in later years there was a court house for the administration of the borough. The 1st Marquis of Bute swept away these inner walls. In this view by Sargent the little girl is sitting on the remains of the wall that connected the keep with the Black Tower on the site of the Roman South Gate. The keep, 'a ruin hoary with age and picturesque with ivy and decay', was known to the Victorians as Iestyn's Tower, after the last Welsh lord of Morgannwg.

6. *In her proud Castle, once Fitzhamon sway'd*
   With iron sceptre, and in pomp display'd
   His Norman banner on her vanquish'd towers;

But now a milder, lighter influence pours
In fostering radiance o'er its wide domains,
And in its halls, the princely Stuart reigns.

(W.L. Jenkins, 1856)

In the fifteenth century Richard Beauchamp, Earl of Warwick, restored the Castle after the depredations of Owain Glyndwr, and built the Octagon Tower in the west wall. Jasper, Earl of Bedford, added the four bays later in that century, and four hundred years later John Mount-Stuart, 1st Marquis of Bute, built the wings shown on either side in this view by Collings circa 1865.

7. In 1893 the south wing was rebuilt by the 3rd Marquis and his architect, William Burges, who created a fairy-tale castle which owed a little to many periods and many cultures. The Octagon Tower was crowned with a graceful lead and timber spire which, with the great Clock Tower to the south, altered the skyline of Cardiff. I treasure the memory of Professor William Rees conducting the Historical Association Conference around the Roman and Norman remains in 1961. A puzzled visitor drew his attention to the Victorian Gothic additions to the west wall, which he had ignored. 'That?' exclaimed the professor. 'That doesn't *exist*!' But he made amends in his *History of the City*.

8. Maxwell Fraser described the interior of Burges' castle as 'a staggering blend of 'curious conceits' and ostentation run riot. It should most certainly be seen,' he added, 'in order to realise what a Victorian architect could do when he had unlimited funds at his disposal.' This Library was formed from the ground floor of the fifteenth century Great Hall, and the date over the door is 1880. Visitors saw only empty shelves when the Castle was given to the citizens of Cardiff by the 5th Marquis in 1947, but gradually they are being filled up again.

9. Originally the Library housed the fine collection of works on ecclesiastical history and architecture amassed by John, 3rd Marquis of Bute, 1847-1900. Though a scholar with a retiring nature, he had also a strong sense of public duty, and was Lord Mayor of Cardiff from 1890 to 1891. A contemporary wrote of the contents of his Library that 'viewed from an aesthetic or a literary point of view, the truly unique collection is a fine reflex of the mind of its noble owner'.

10. The Summer Smoking Room crowns a suite of bachelor apartments in the Clock Tower, exhibiting, in the words of J.P. Grant, 'a wealth of taste and learning'. Carvings over the fireplace illustrate the summer amusements of lovers, though, beneath the central figure of Cupid and a love-bird, matrimony is depicted as two leashed hounds pulling in opposite directions! The candelabra over the table represents the sun and its rays, its light reflected in the bevelled mirrors lining the dome above the clerestory gallery, just glimpsed in this view of 1923, when the Marquis was in residence and the Castle fully furnished.

11. Outside, the Clock Tower (built between 1867 and 1872) was equally ornate, its lead roof dotted with stars of pure tin. This view shows how closely the mediaeval town had been built to the protection of the Castle. The Angel Inn, on the right, was demolished in 1882. The shadow on the left is a puzzle. Is it of a child? No. 24 shows the effect of figures moving during the lengthy exposure of a photographic plate, but here there is no substance to the shadow. Many a ghost story must have been based on evidence like this in the early days of photography.

12. This view from the Clock Tower before 1877 shows the High Street, St. John's Church and, in the distance, the masts of sailing ships in the docks. Houses are crowded right up to the main gate of the Castle and, bottom centre, a 'middle row' (shown on John Speed's map of 1610) divides Castle Street from Angel Street. These extra rows, fitted into former open spaces, were a feature of the old walled town and were gradually cleared away during the later nineteenth century.

13. Taken by E.W.M. Corbett about 1870, this photograph shows the Castle main gate beside the Black Tower, traditionally the place of imprisonment of Robert, Duke of Normandy, from 1126 until his death in 1134. In actual fact, the Black Tower was built by Gilbert de Clare in the late thirteenth century, so Robert could only have been imprisoned in the Keep. The early afternoon sun casts the shadow of a Duke Street chimney on High Corner House, the office of Lord Bute's solicitor. Built in the seventeenth century, it was demolished in 1877.

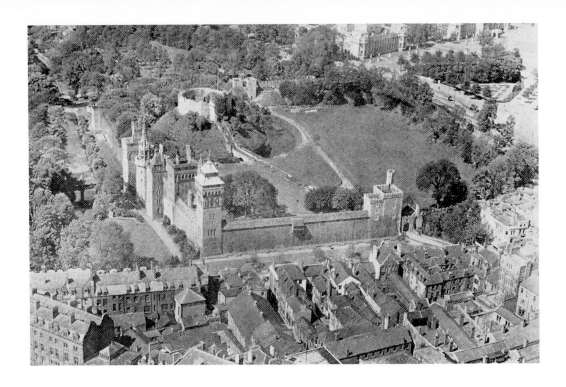

14. This aerial view, taken about 1920, shows the result of the clearance of houses below the south-west wall rebuilt by Burges between 1865 and 1870. He incorporated many Norman defensive features, including the timber hourd mid-way along the wall. Such a structure would have protected the defenders while giving them a vantage point from which to repel besiegers at the foot of the wall. Now there are trees beside the main gate and flower beds below the battlements, but Castle and City, old and new, remain in close proximity. Travel-writers like H.V. Morton found the contrast particularly striking – 'A city that has grown up out of an age of steam and machinery preserves in its centre a vivid memory of an age of swords.'

Cardiff Castle.

15. One of a series of colour cards printed in Germany, which then led the field in photo-litho techniques, this postcard shows several interesting details – the vines planted by the 3rd Marquis in 1875, the window-cleaner's cart (by marchesal appointment?), and the bill-board advertising a fête in the Castle grounds. The animals along the wall were carved by Nicholls and Antrill between 1887 and 1900. While approving the sea-lion, lynx, monkeys, pelican and bear, the Marquis considered the lions bearing his arms on the gate-pillars 'to be too modest in demeanour, savouring rather of pets'. Between the two world wars the animal wall was moved to the west of the tower and has recently been refurbished.

Cardiff Castle, from St. John's Tower

Valentines Series

16. This sepia card, postmarked 1905 and taken in the opposite direction to No. 12, shows how the houses had been cleared from in front of the vine-clad south-west wall though they still crowded the Castle on the south-east. The imaginative reconstruction undertaken by Burges for the 3rd Marquis ended at the Black Tower in the centre of the picture.

17. This wider view, also from St. John's Tower, was taken in 1923. The Keep has been cleared of creeper and undergrowth, and behind it to the right is the reconstructed North Roman Gate. In the middle-distance, one side of Duke Street has been demolished and the south-east wall is being rebuilt on the original Roman foundations now preserved in a corridor that runs through the north, east and south-east walls of the Castle enclosure.

18. Ernest T. Bush was the publisher of this view of Duke Street from the junction of North Road (later Kingsway), Queen Street and St. John's Square. Here until the late eighteenth century Cardiff Corporation promoted the 'sport' of baiting a bull with mastiffs. Professor Rees suggested the resurrection of the old name of 'The Bullring' for 'the City's central point' but nothing was done. The 4th Marquis bought up and demolished the properties on the right-hand (Castle) side of Duke Street to relieve the congestion and to reveal the Roman wall.

19. There is congestion of a different kind in this *Daily Mail* photograph taken in the opposite direction in 1927, when the work had been completed. The crowds have been brought on to the gaily decorated streets by the Royal visit. Most of the ladies wear fashionable cloche hats, and the policeman has exchanged the pill-box cap of the previous generation for a helmet. We can see on the left how the Marquis, ever attentive to historical detail, has had the blue lias of the original Roman wall outlined with a band of red Radyr stone and the work continued in carboniferous 'mountain' limestone to differentiate for future generations between original and reconstruction.

RIVER TAFF, SHEWING CARDIFF CASTLE.

20. This colour card, printed in Bavaria, shows Cardiff Bridge, downstream from the original crossing. 'The course of ye water in this River is so swift, and bringeth such Logs and Bodies from the Woodie Hills,' wrote Holinshed in 1557, 'that they do not seldom crush the Bridge in pieces.' Time and again he was proved correct, though it was ice after the sudden thaw of January 1795 that caused the change of site. This bridge with its stone piers and elaborate iron parapets was built between 1876 and 1878 and widened in 1931. In Bute Park, behind the Castle Lodge in the centre of the picture, lie the ruins of the monastery of the Blackfriars, inhabited as late as 1830 by a Taff coracle fisher.

21. Earlier bridges carried the road from the west over the Taff and through the West Gate of the walled town. Excavations prior to the rebuilding of this gateway in 1921 revealed three different levels of pebbled road surface. No. 14 shows the overgrown rubble at the foot of the Octagon and Herbert Towers which was all that remained of the original gate, sited where attackers would have to brave fifty yards of fire from the Castle wall should they succeed in forcing the town gate.

22. 'This towne,' wrote Rice Merrick in 1578, 'is environned with a faire high wall... with four faire Gates... On the Towne wall, was builded a Towre, called Cockestoure, to defend the Towne against the danger of the Sea.' Until the 1960's fragments of the town wall could be seen on the banks of the Glamorganshire Canal, constructed in 1794 along the old town ditch. Cock's Tower, shown here, proved an obstruction to the barges, which often swung out and struck the opposite bank. This portion was filled in to form part of Hill's Terrace, and now the name 'Town Wall' ('Mur y Dref') is given to one arm of St. David's Centre, where its course is outlined on the floor in contrasting stone. The only remaining fragment of the Town Wall beside the south-east bastion of the Castle can be seen in No. 85.

23. Until the cutting of the Glamorganshire Canal, mule trains carried coal from the mines to coastal vessels moored at the Town Quay. The Taff is, of course, a tidal river and the combination of sea and river flood frequently threatened the town until 1850, when Isambard Kingdom Brunel made the 'new cut' which diverted the Taff from the old Town Quay and created new land for the railway, for Cardiff Arms Park and for Temperance Town (now the Central Bus Station and Central Square). Westgate Street follows the old course of the Taff, and Quay Street, shown here about 1890, still leads from High Street to the site of the old quay.

24. By walking a few yards from the view of St. John's Tower from Quay Street, the photographer could glimpse the Clock Tower over the rooftops of Womanby Street. The name, recorded as 'Hundmanby' in 1270 and 'Home-and-bye-Street' in 1780, comes from the old Norse for 'huntsman's dwelling'. A trading post was probably established here by the Vikings in those dark years between the withdrawal of the Romans and the Norman Conquest. The chapel, founded in 1696 as the first Nonconformist place of worship in Cardiff, was rebuilt after a fire in 1847, and in 1889 its congregation amalgamated with another to build a chapel completed in 1894 in Cowbridge Road, where it is still known as 'New' Trinity.

25. The contrast between the ethereal beauty of Cardiff's towers and the drabness of her back streets
is illustrated in these three photographs (23, 24, 25) taken in 1890-1891. The town is particularly well
documented for these years as the result of a survey sponsored by the Free Libraries Committee and
the Photographic Society. The original pictures, with many additions, are preserved in Cardiff Central
Library. Womanby Street and Quay Street are still recognisable, though a multi-story car park has
replaced the small shops on the right in No. 23. Evans Court in North Street (No. 25) was demolished
shortly after 1891 and the site is now included in the broad sweep of Kingsway (No. 68).

26. In 1880 Thomas Glyde noted that a few small town houses still remained in the oldest part of the Borough around Womanby Street, Church Street and High Street. They were 'a small class of low cottage property' originally thatched. There is a remarkable survival of early nineteenth century housing in Jones Court, off Womanby Street. This row of six workers' cottages, built in the 1830's with one room up, one down, were shared between eight families in 1841, with common cess-pits and no running water. They were restored to their original appearance by Lock-Necrews Hill and Partners and in 1982 won a Prince of Wales Award. In this reconstruction we see them, not in the run-down condition produced by years of over-crowding, but as they appeared when first built.

Church Street, Cardiff

27. Church Street, glimpsed in the background of No. 23, is alive with people in their summer wear on this colour card postmarked 1908, and the cart is about to pass a hansom cab drawn up to the pavement, centre right. Not far from this spot the Protestant martyr Rawlins White was burned to death in 1555. 124 years later two Roman Catholic priests, Philip Evans and John Lloyd, were dragged through these streets to a traitor's death. Over it all, the tower of St. John's watched serenely.

28. In 1578 Rice Merrick described St. John's tower as 'a very faire Steeple of grey Ashlere... the workman-shipp of it, being carryed to a great heighth, and above beautified with Pinnacles, of all skilfull behoulders is very well liked of'. It had been built in 1473, the gift of Lady Anne Neville, wife of Richard Duke of Gloucester, later King Richard III. The view by A. Freke was taken in 1910 from the Library, opposite is 'Howells & Company' general store, and the carts are drawing up outside the covered market in Trinity Street.

29. Though the pinnacles of St. John's tower point heavenwards, its foundations have always been very much part of the town and its bustling life. The fire engine was kept beneath it from 1739 to 1818, before the building of 'Cardiff Fire Engine Station' close to old Town Hall. Here Cardiff Fire Brigade pose in front of their horse-drawn fire engine, still in use in the 1880's.

30. The church of St. John the Baptist was founded in the thirteenth century; a new chancel, nave and two aisles were built in 1443 after the sack of Cardiff by Owain Glyndwr, and the tower was added in 1473. St. John's was originally a daughter church of St. Mary's on the banks of the Taff, destroyed after the great flood of 1607 broke through the churchyard wall. Though St. Mary's was rebuilt in Bute Street in 1843 (with Wordsworth contributing a sonnet for fund-raising), St. John's had long been the parish church of the upper town, and is the venue for the Assize Service and other colourful civic events. 'In a country less rich in antiquities than this,' wrote the American consul Wirt Sykes in 1880, 'St. John's Church would be an enormous lion.'

31. The constrast between these pictures shows the extent of the alterations of 1898/99 when the chancel was given a pitched roof, a south porch was added, and the vestries were extended to the road. At the same time, a pathway was made across the churchyard to link Working Street with Trinity Street, where the old Vicarage once stood. The locations of the levelled graves were marked with brass letters, some of which still remain in the path. Hawkers and street musicians still find 'sanctuary' here and ply their trade on church ground.

32. In the north aisle chapel of St. John's lie the effigies of the brothers Sir William and Sir John Herbert. Their family became Lords of Cardiff and Earls of Pembroke and were prominent in South Wales history, though there was more repetition of Christian names than was usual even in those days and 16 Williams in their family tree are calculated to confuse local historians! They were typical of the gentry who enriched themselves by the purchase of monastic land after the Dissolution, and one branch of the family was involved with the adventurers who gave Cardiff the reputation of 'a nest of piracie' at the very time that Sir John was secretary to Queen Elizabeth I.

33. 'Without the North Gate,' reported Rice Merric in 1578, 'Gilbert de Clare... founded the Gray ffryers, wherein Sir William Herbert, Knight, hath builded a house of late.' The stones of the Franciscan Friary (said to contain the bodies of Llewelyn Bren and his persecutor, Sir William Flemyng) were used to build the Herbert House in what is now Greyfriars Road. Its ruins, photographed by G.H. Wills in 1888, were demolished in 1958, despite protests from many Cardiff citizens, and the Pearl Assurance Building, Cardiff's first and tallest skyscraper, now occupies the site. In its entrance hall is a sketch-plan of the old Friary.

34. When the British Association of Science met at Cardiff in 1891, delegates who expected coal tips and the murk of an industrial atmosphere were reported to be astonished at the clean air and beauty of the town. This study, published by the *Illustrated London News* to mark the occasion, conveys the contrast between the Cardiff of the past, epitomised by the Castle and St. John's, and what was to be Cardiff's future – its Dockland.

35. The dock and basin on the left of the panorama opposite were those built by the 2nd Marquis and opened in 1839. The lock and basin of the Glamorganshire Canal were too far from deep water and had proved totally inadequate for the larger ships necessary for the increased iron trade. The Bute West Dock, 19½ acres in extent, cost the Marquis nearly a quarter of a million pounds in cash with another £137,000 in materials from his estates. It was an imaginative investment, and to his initiative Cardiff owed nearly a hundred years of prosperity. At first the docks were crowded with sail, as in the sketch above.

Copyright.

36. As trade expanded and sail gave way to steam for the shipping of coal, the Bute East Dock and Basin were constructed in 1855 by the Bute trustees during the minority of the 3rd Marquis. By the time these coloured postcards were published, the Pierhead Building has been erected in 1896 between the two Bute Docks.

37. The offices of the Bute Docks Company, the Pier Head Building was designed in French Gothic style by William Frame, who had assisted both William Burges at the Castle and John Prichard at Llandaff Cathedral. True to their tradition of architectural exuberance, he mixed gargoyles and pinnacles with a cluster of hexagonal chimneys over the large panel on the west front where the arms of the Borough and of Bute are carved between a ship and a locmotive, with the motto *Trwy Ddwr a Thân'* – 'By Water and Fire'.

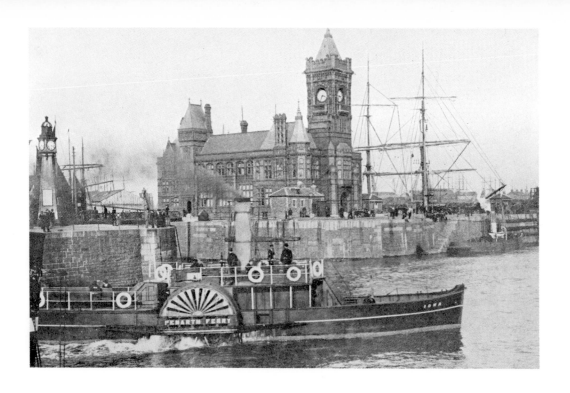

38. Three steam ferries, 'Kate', 'Iona' and 'Belle Marie' plied between Penarth Beach and Docks and Cardiff Pierhead, where they linked with a horse-bus service to the Castle. They were not always necessary. The *South Wales Coal Annual* for 1909-1910 reported proudly that customs officers were able to cross the estuary from ship to ship, so busy were the Docks. Be that as it may (and it resembles the folk legend of squirrels leaping from tree to tree across wooded South Wales), the 'Iona' is pictured here leaving the Bute Steps at the Pier Head. A tug is moored close to the entrance to Bute East Dock, and there are tall ships in the docks and basin.

39. Cardiff and Penarth Docks were built on either side of the estuary of the Rivers Taff and Ely, in the shelter of Penarth Head. This Frith postcard shows how Dockland had become built up in the background of this cluster of pilot boats and ferries. Tall-masted sailing ships are still using the Docks, but there is a steamer in the Dry Dock on the left, opened in 1897.

40. Cardiff Channel Dry Docks and Pontoon Company spanned the estuary with the Dry Docks opening direct from the channel on the east bank, and the Pontoon on the west bank, nearer Penarth. When John Ballinger wrote his *Guide to Cardiff* in 1908, the pneumatic tools being demonstrated here to a trio of bowler-hatted docksmen were the marvel of the works. 'Under the guidance of a single man,' he commented, 'the amount of work which can be done in this way is simply astonishing.'

41. Incorporated in 1882, the Mountstuart Dry Docks grew from the single Graving Dock privately opened in 1872 into a massive undertaking capable of handling the largest ships of the day. The company was particularly proud of working conditions in the Blacksmiths' Shop pictured here. *The atmosphere of this great shop is worthy of note, for in spite of the long row of blacksmiths' fires there is an entire absence of smoke and sulphur. Every smith's fire is fitted with a patent exhaust fan which carries off all smoke and gases from each individual fire, leaving the atmosphere not only clear of smoke, but free from objectionable fumes of every kind.*

42. In these days of mechanisation, it is easy to forget that it was the labour and sweat of the navvy and the horse which built Cardiff's Dockland. The hand shovel and the wooden cart were the predecessors of the great bulldozers which are now demolishing acres of warehouses like these constructed at 'Ely Harbour, Cardiff' only a century ago.

43. When the labour was complete, came the moment of pomp and pageantry. The last and largest of Cardiff's docks was named after Queen Alexandra. In this City Hall painting by W. Hatherell, the Queen looks on from the carriage as King Edward VII knights the Lord Mayor of Cardiff, Alderman William Smith Crossman, after the opening of Queen Alexandra Dock on 13th July 1907.

44. Roath Dock (opened in 1887) and Queen Alexandra Dock completed the complex which built Cardiff into the premier coal port in the world, reaching its peak in 1913, when 13,677,000 tons of coal were exported. Such intense activity necessitated building on a grand scale, as in the Docks Post Office. In the crowd of men outside, long overcoats and bowlers or top hats distinguish the 'docksmen' from the lounging dockers in their cloth caps, and the seamen waiting hopefully for a ship.

45. The Cardiff docksmen or merchants (according to J. Kyrle Fletcher from Newport) 'combine the caution of a Scot with the shrewdness of the Tynesider, and the cunning of the devil himself'. The centre of their activity was the Coal Exchange, Mountstuart Square, built between 1883 and 1886. Its scale can be gauged by the length of the extending ladders on the left. Inside, the main hall was redesigned in 1911 and refurbished in 1978/79 in readiness for a Welsh Assembly, rejected by the referendum of 1st March 1979. A political miscalculation prolonged the life of this magnificent building.

46. Vital to the development of the docks was the railway system which by the 1870's had displaced the canal for the carriage of heavy goods. The Taff Vale Railway opened the first section of its line to Abercynon in 1840 and extended it to Merthyr within six months. In 1845 a Royal Charter was granted for the South Wales Railway to link Gloucester with Cardiff and the west, and other branch lines followed, all to be amalgamated in 1921 as the Great Western Railway. 'The present station for passenger traffic,' wrote W.L. Jenkins in 1854, 'is in Crockherbtown, about a mile from the terminus.' This was the small station pictured by Collings before its rebuilding in 1887.

47. The name Crockherbtown for the suburb outside the East Gate was changed in 1886 to Queen Street, in honour of Victoria and as an extension of the old Queen Street between St. John's Square and the Friary. In 1887 the newly named Queen Street Station and offices were rebuilt in Victorian Gothic. Along the platform stone heads (past station masters or recalcitrant passengers?) looked down from the corbels on which rested graceful wrought iron arches. This splendid structure, seen here decorated for the Royal Visit of 1912, was replaced by British Rail with some undistinguished boxes as entrance and booking office, and a modern office block on this site for the Automobile Association — perhaps an ironic comment on changes in transport?

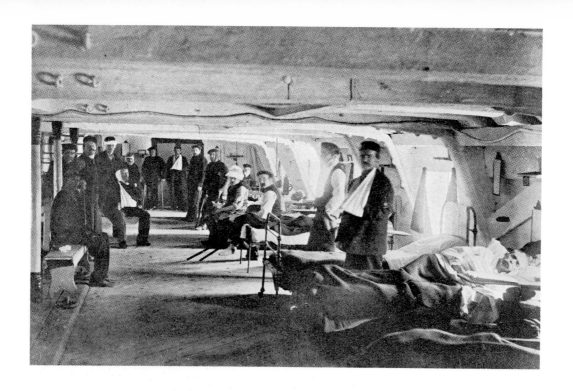

48. *The Hamadryad,* a man of war of 46 guns, 1,000 tons, was built at Pembroke Dock in 1823 for the reserve fleet, but never saw action. A painting in the City Hall shows her being towed up the estuary in 1866. She was finally moored on the little peninsula between the Taff and the Sea Lock of the Glamorganshire Canal, where she served as a seamen's hospital, financed by a levy of two shillings on every ship entering the port, and providing free treatment to seamen irrespective of nationality. The name, the ship's bell and her figurehead are preserved in the permanent hospital building close by. The old *Hamadryad* was sold in 1905 and towed to Bideford to be broken up.

49. In medical and social care 'self-help' was the principle advocated by the Victorians, and many friendly societies provided a measure of security for their members in days of hardship. When times were better, they brightened the streets with their uniforms, bands and banners. Cardiff Hibernian Society is seen here on parade in 1892.

50. The development of the Docks brought a vast number of people into the new suburbs built on the low-lying land between the old walled town and the sea, and west of Cardiff Bridge into Canton. There was a serious outbreak of cholera in 1849, and the provisions of the Public Health Act were extended to Cardiff in 1850 after an inspector of the Board of Health had reported that 'nothing can be worse than the house accommodation provided for the labouring classes and the poor of the town, and the overcrowding is fearful'. Even when attempts were made to relieve this situation, hurriedly-built houses deteriorated rapidly, as in this 1892 photograph of Halket (later Avon) Street, only recently demolished in Canton.

51. The population of Cardiff doubled between 1851 and 1871, and again by 1881. Between 1881 and 1902 20,000 houses were built in Cardiff. Emerald Street in Roath was typical of this late nineteenth century building with its corner shops and throngs of children, some barefoot, whose only playground was the streets.

Queen Street, Cardiff

C. 1059

52. In contrast, the commercial life of the town revolved around the two main streets, where individual shopkeepers vied with one another to build higher and more ornately than their neighbour, and where the big stores have gradually expanded over the little shops of the mid-nineteenth century. There are many contrasts of height and style in this view-card of Queen Street from the junction with Park Place. It also shows the mixture of mechanised and horse-drawn transport which characterised the Cardiff scene after the introduction of electric trams in 1902. A tram is approaching, but horses still have the monopoly of the delivery of goods.

Queen St.   Cardiff

53. This unusual colour card was printed in Saxony for the Milton Artlette Series. It shows Queen Street from the west, probably on a Sunday for the blinds are drawn in the shop windows and the street is almost empty. There was a craving for novelty among the publishers of picture postcards and in 1904 a new technique was introduced from the Continent for a series on theatre stars, and was soon extended to viewcards like this. The lines of the principal buildings are 'jewelled', i.e. picked out in glitter, which gives a pretty effect in colour but can become blurred in a black and white reproduction. The smaller building slightly left of centre with the glass canopy is the old Empire Theatre.

54. Beyond Queen Street lies Newport Road, where ploughing matches had taken place in the fields alongside the Old Infirmary as late as 1850. By the time this colour card was printed, Newport Road had block paving and tram lines. However, as in the last card, the overhead wires are missing, so this may be a case of the printer either introducing an interesting vehicle into a genuine view, or blocking out the wires for artistic effect.

55. 'Roath Road' Wesleyan Church, seen in the background of No. 54 and of this photograph, retained the old name of Newport Road. The foundation stone was laid in 1870, but the church was destroyed by bombing in 1941, the ruins were cleared in 1955, and a high-rise block of offices stands in its place. In the foreground are the church and school of St. James the Great, a daughter church of the parish of St. John's. It had been erected in 1894, two years before this photograph, to replace the iron church which first served the growing population in the area to the east, taken into the Borough in 1875.

56. Cardiff's first hospital is remembered only in the name of the 'Spital Building' No. 130 Queen Street, but the Infirmary was sited in this building just beyond the Taff Railway bridge in Newport Road from its foundation in 1824 until 1881. By the time of this picture, the Old Infirmary had become the first University College (see No. 86).

57. Owing to 'the phenomenal growth of the town and district', a larger Infirmary building was established here at Longcross, or Payn's Cross, in 1881. Over the years extensions have been added in a jumble of contrasting styles. The policeman is wearing a similar type of uniform cap to his colleague in No. 18. Despite his watchful attitude, what little traffic there is has halted for everyone to gaze at the novelty of a street photographer.

58. In the right angle formed by the main shopping centres of Queen Street/Duke Street and High Street/St. Mary Street lay the heart of the old Borough. Ebenezer Calvinistic Methodist Church had been founded here in 1828 near Paradise Place (perhaps an old monastery garden) on what was then open ground — too far, the minister thought, from 'the town'. Soon it was surrounded by row upon row of small houses opening directly on to the pavements, and was twice enlarged to accommodate its growing congregation. Workmen demolishing Ebenezer in 1978 disturbed the remains of cholera victims from the epidemic of 1849. St. David's Centre covers this area to-day and the fountain outside Marks and Spencer's is on the site of Ebenezer.

Mr. Edgar Fawckner.
Architect

Salem Welsh C.M. Church, Canton.
Front Elevation.

Mr James Stephens
Builder.

59. Chapel building in Cardiff varied from the relatively simple rectangular box of Ebenezer to the extravagance of Crwys Road Presbyterian, from the massively classical Tabernacle, The Hayes, to the mildly Gothic Salem Calvinistic Methodist, Canton. Built in 1856 and enlarged in 1868, Salem was distinguished not by its architecture but by the energy of its congregation. It was noted for the strength of its Sunday School (rated by the number of prizes in the annual examination) and the excellence of its music, led by Madam Clara Novello Davies, mother of Ivor Novello. These activities were celebrated in a series of postcards presented to their minister in 1911.

60. In 1882 a building for the Free Library, Town Museum and Craft and Arts School was erected in Trinity Street (No. 28). Trinity Chapel, which once occupied the site, can be seen behind St. John's in No. 12. Eventually the building was given over entirely to books and manuscripts and was extended in 1896. The new south façade, shown here, is crowned with a massive bust of Minerva, goddess of wisdom. She looks out across The Hayes, so called from the hedges which once divided the gardens of the houses within the town wall.

61. For more than fifty years street traders plied their wares on Hayes Island. Numerous bye-laws prohibited 'quacks and cheapjacks' and tried to confine the stands to those traders 'who will conduct their business quietly'. Despite the efforts of the Corporation, the shrill cries of the barrow boys and the strains of street musicians would penetrate the reverential hush preserved in the reference and research rooms. The latter, shown here, was for a generation the particular preserve of T.J. Hopkins, who had an intuitive sense of the whereabouts of any particular manuscript requested, and an enthusiasm for local history particularly of the Vale of Glamorgan.

62. Wharton Street links The Hayes with St. Mary Street, which now runs without a break into High Street, seen here in 1928. At one time they were separated by the Guildhall just where the photographer must have been standing at the junction with Quay Street and Church Street. The last hall on this site was demolished in 1861 and with it a stone tablet in memory of Rawlins White 'fisherman of this parish... burnt at the stake for his religion's sake, 1555'. Foxe's *Book of Martyrs* contains an eye-witness account by another Cardiff man, John Dane.

63. One of the corbels carved in 1887 in the chancel of St. John's represents Rawlins White. In 1912 'two Protestants of this town' provided the bronze tablet pictured here. It was fixed on the façade of Bethany Baptist Church in Wharton Street and there it remains, even though the church has been demolished and its gallery and arches have been incorporated into James Howell's store (No. 28). The principles and sufferings of Rawlins White seem far removed from the world of gentlemen's fashion which surrounds the memorial to-day!

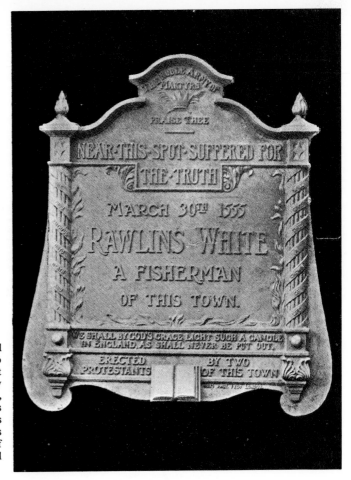

St. Mary Street, Cardiff

Valentines Series

64. This sepia card in the Valentine series shows the south end of St. Mary Street when trams trundled beside the hansom cabs. It was named after the old parish church which stood about the centre of the picture until washed away by the Taff floods in the seventeenth century. The town houses of the gentry once lined St. Mary Street and it was the main thoroughfare of the old Borough — 'Here walked and preached Wesley: here walked martyrs and murderers, cut-throats, pirates, guildsmen, monks... through the South Gate they might come to trade, smuggle, bargain or pray. Burgesses and Radicals... devils and divines. You and me.' (Peter Leech, *View Around Cardiff*, 1969.)

65. The 1890 extension to the Royal Hotel (centre right in the previous picture) was the scene of a dramatic rescue in 1914. Winnie Jones, a maid at the hotel, was trapped by fire at the marked window. The firemen's ladders, on the left above the corner building, could reach only to the fifth floor. A young workman, Walter Cleall, was passing when he heard her cries for help. He forced his way through the smoke, but emerged at the wrong window. Undeterred, he worked his way along the parapet to the girl's room and persuaded her to climb out with him and edge her way back to safety. The rescue ended in their romance and marriage, and admiring local traders showered them with wedding gifts.

66. In 1853 this Town Hall in St. Mary Street replaced the Guild Hall shown in old prints in the middle of the High Street. Designed in heavy classical style by Horace Jones, the Town Hall complex included 'the Old Town Hall, the Old Post Office, the Police Court and Parade Ground, the Fire Brigade Offices and Rate Offices, having a frontage to St. Mary Street of 211 feet, to Westgate Street 212 feet' (*Town Hall Sale Catalogue,* 1907). It was from here that the city status of Cardiff was proclaimed on 23rd October 1905.

67. This colour postcard depicts the new arms of the city. On the shield a red dragon rampant supports, in front of a leek, a banner with the arms borne by the last Welsh Prince of Morgannwg and by the Lords of Cardiff and of Glamorgan. The supporters are a Welsh goat representing the mountains and a hippocamp, or sea-horse, representing the sea, the twin sources of Cardiff's prosperity. By a special Royal Warrant, the city was allowed to adopt as its crest 'a Tudor Rose on three ostrich feathers, argent, issuing out of a Mural Crown proper'. Thus the history, status, and future national significance of Cardiff were encapsulated in the new City Arms.

68. The new city deserved a new civic centre, and sites were considered in 'Cardiff Arms' Park and near the G.W.R. Station, before the choice fell on the Marquis of Bute's gardens in Cathays Park (the reference is again to hayes or hedges and, by implication, the gardens within them; so Cathays was Kate's garden or 'Cate's Hayes' in its earliest recorded form in 1682). This photograph, taken from the old Town Hall looking towards the new, shows Kingsway leading to the Law Courts and City Hall, with the eastern wall of the Castle still under construction on the left.

69. The Civic Centre built of Portland stone had considerable impact on contemporary architects. J.B. Hilling *Cardiff and the Valleys,* 1973, quotes the reaction of Professor Reilly: 'It seemed at the time like a new revelation... everyone who could afford it flocked to Cardiff and came back enthralled.' In 1897 E.A. Rickards beat 55 other competitors with his design for both the Law Courts and City Hall.

Cardiff. The New Law Courts. No. 10.

70. The harmony created by the placing of dissimilar Portland stone buildings in open green spaces has continued to exercise its fascination. In the University College Centenary Book, *Fountains of Praise* (1983), Dewi-Prys Thomas described the impact on him as a young student in 'sooted exile' in the north and coming to Cathays Park in the September sunlight of 1934: 'All those noble buildings shone in mellow harmonies of white. Of differing styles they sang united in concord of tone values... the qualities of space between the noble buildings as important as the quality of the buildings themselves.'

71. After winning the competition, Rickards redesigned the dome and tower of the City Hall in baroque style and on a grander scale. The first of the Cathays Park's dragons (by H.C. Fehr) snarls from the top of the dome. The foundation stone of the City Hall was laid in October 1901 and it was officially opened by the Marquis of Bute in 1906. This photograph was taken after the erection of Sir Goscombe John's statue of Lord Tredegar in 1909. The Museum site is still empty, but there is a glimpse of the front of University College among the trees behind the statue.

72. The entrance to the City Hall is through a *porte cochère* into a plain bathstone hall from which staircases rise on either side to the marble hall with its paired Siena columns. Above the staircases were niches and between the bronze rails were pedestals which seemed to Mr. J.L. Wheatley, Town Clerk for the past 37 years, 'to clamour for embellishment'.

73. He consulted Mr. D.A. Thomas (later Lord Rhondda) who agreed to donate ten statues representing the chief figures in Welsh history. A competition was held to see whose list could nearest approach the ten selected by a committee of 'three eminent Welshmen'. The *Western Mail* then published biographical sketches of the chosen ten and on these the various sculptors based their interpretations. Boadicea was added to fill another pedestal. In this photograph of the right hand staircase the chosen figures are – on the left, Llewelyn the Last, in the niche in in the background, William Williams, Pantecelyn, the hymn writer; on the right, Sir Thomas Picton and Owain Glyndwr, and nearest the camera, Harri Tewdwr, later Henry VII.

74. In contrast to the cool marble spaces of the rest of the City Hall, the Council Chamber, apart from the four massive columns supporting the dome, is panelled in oak inlaid with holly, and the circular oak seating is upholstered in rich claret leather. Behind the Lord Mayor's chair the outer columns of oak support models of sailing ships representing the port of Cardiff. In this photograph the Lord Mayor is transferring the deeds of the National Museum to Lord Mostyn, President of its Council. The Lady Mayoress, the Mace bearers, Clerk (J.L. Wheatley) and councillors seem aware of the dignity of the occasion, but what are the thoughts of the gentleman twirling his moustaches on the left of the picture?

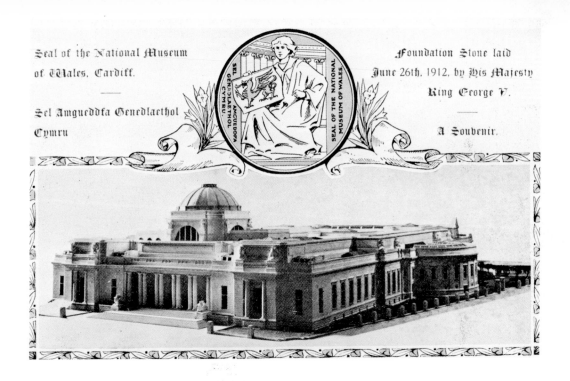

Seal of the National Museum of Wales, Cardiff.

Sel Amgueddfa Genedlaethol Cymru

SEAL OF THE NATIONAL MUSEUM OF WALES

SEL AMGUEDDFA GENEDLAETHOL CYMRU

Foundation Stone laid June 26th, 1912, by His Majesty King George V.

A Souvenir.

75. The building of the National Museum of Wales was delayed by the outbreak of the First World War and the quadrangular plan of the model in this souvenir postcard is still not complete. The usual design competition, this time with 130 entries, was won by Smith and Brewer. The chief feature of their restrained design is the dome and the octagonal lantern gallery below it casts a pink light on the marble columns and floor of the main hall far below. Although the foundation stone was laid in 1912 and the first part opened in 1927, the eastern wing and the Reardon-Smith Lecture Theatre were not completed until 1932.

76. King George V, who had laid the foundation stone 15 years before, was at last able to perform the opening ceremony on 21st April 1927. The inscription on the left of the main door is in English and Welsh, in keeping with the declared aim of the Museum to 'teach the world about Wales, and the Welsh people about their own fatherland'.

77. Outside the crowds waited. It was a scene of pageantry with the immaculate lines of the guard of honour and military band drawn up in front of the Museum steps. A human touch was added by a group of veterans, in various stages of formal and informal dress, who gathered to greet the mascot of their old regiment.

assemblée du „Gorsedd" ou Collège des Bardes de Grande-Bretagne, à Cardiff (Pays de Galles)
Discours de „Taldir" l'un des 20 délégués bretons.

78. 'Assembly of the 'Gorsedd' or College of the Bards of Great Britain at Cardiff (Wales). Discourse of 'Taldir' one of twenty Breton delegates.' This French postcard commemorates the first visit of the National Eisteddfod to Cardiff in 1899.

79. 'In front of the National Museum building,' wrote J. Kyrle Fletcher, 'is a flower garden, and on the green turf is a circle of rough unhewn stones, the Gorsedd Circle of the Bards of the Island of Britain. It was here that the National Eisteddfod was proclaimed, with pomp and strange ritual, when it was held in Cardiff.' There is another stone circle in the Castle Grounds. On a return visit in 1976 the City had become too congested for the expected crowds and the Eisteddfod was held at Pentwyn on its eastern boundary. The caption on this card is, of course, incorrect; by the time the Gorsedd Gardens were laid out in 1909, Cardiff had become a city. It is unusual to see a view of this east side of the City Hall, but the Museum had not then been built.

80. When this card was printed, Cardiff had only one civic war memorial standing between the Law Courts and City Hall. After nearly half a century without a major war, the country had been shaken by the hostilities in South Africa, but no thought of another war entered the mind of this caption-writer. 'The' War Memorial, designed by Alfred Toft, bears the names of nearly 200 Welshmen 'who fell in South Africa, 1899-1902' and over them is the winged figure of Peace.

81. In the First World War 272,924 Welshmen enlisted. Many of them were recruited at centres like Cardiff's Neptune Inn. 'THE WELCH REGT. YOUNG MEN... JOIN AT ONCE.' 'COME ALONG BOYS, ENLIST TODAY.' 'YOUR KING AND COUNTRY NEED YOU TO MAINTAIN THE HONOUR AND GLORY OF THE BRITISH EMPIRE.' 'FALL IN. ANSWER NOW IN YOUR COUNTRY'S HOUR OF NEED.' 'Why are *you* stopping HERE when your pals are out THERE?' 'WELSH GUARDS RECRUITS – GWYR IEUAINC.' 'THIS WAY TO THE FRONT. THE 3rd BATT. THE WELCH REGIMENT is sending drafts TO THE FRONT EVERY WEEK. Your comrades in arms are appealing to you...' The Book of Remembrance of the First World War contains 35,000 names.

82. The Welsh National War Memorial was designed by H.N. (later Sir Ninian) Comper as a circular sunken court within a colonade of Portland stone. Above the central fountain the bronze figure of a soldier, a sailor and an airman (by A. Bertram Pegram) each lift a wreath towards the Messenger of Victory, his sword held up like a cross. Inside is the English inscription composed by Sir Henry Newbolt, and on the outer frieze a dedication in Welsh 'To the Sons of Wales who gave themselves in the War of 1916-1918.' It was commissioned in 1924 but the 'Ceremony of Unveiling and Dedication' by the Prince of Wales (later King Edward VIII) did not take place until 12th June 1928.

83. One reason for the delay was the difficulty of siting the memorial, which finally came to rest in the centre of Alexandra Gardens, a position so perfectly suited to it that the rest of the Civic Centre might have been planned around it, though the reverse was true. This aerial view of 1920 shows (top left) part of the great rectangle bounded on the west by Glamorgan County Hall and the University of Wales Registry (the first building on the site, 1903/04), on the south by the Law Courts, City Hall and Museum, and on the east by University College. Greyfriars can be glimpsed middle right.

84. These two views show the Civic Centre as it might have been — but never was. The Welsh National War Memorial was designed to stand on the circular green outside the City Hall, as shown here. This photograph and a similar one showing circular scaffolding on the same spot have caused a great deal of puzzlement since they were unearthed from a drawer in the Library of the National Museum. Further research solved the problem, at least in part. A small cut-out of Comper's winning design had been slotted into a view of the site and then rephotographed to gauge the effect. Here the English inscription is on the outside, the Welsh inside, an arrangement reversed on the completed memorial.

85. Both the City Council and the Museum authorities objected to the proposed siting on the grounds that it would interfere with the fine effect achieved by the wide, uncluttered frontage of the existing buildings. An alternative site was suggested in the Priory Gardens, but this was opposed by the Marquis of Bute because of a stipulation in the conveyance of the land that no buildings should be erected near his father's statue. Finally, the present site in Alexandra Gardens (No. 83) was approved and building began in 1925.

THE PRINCE OF WALES LAYING FOUNDATION STONE
OF NEW UNIVERSITY COLLEGE CARDIFF, JUNE 28, 05

86. Wearing the robes of Chancellor of the University of Wales, George V (then Prince of Wales) laid the foundation stone of the new University College building on a five-acre site on the east side of Cathays Park. He can be seen at the extreme right of the group on the dais, Bishop Prichard Hughes of Llandaff on the left. Previously the College had been housed in the old Infirmary building in Newport Road (No. 56). Town and gown were close in those early days, for Cardiff had fought hard for the privilege of obtaining the first University College in South Wales, and high and low had contributed to the cause.

87. 'New College' was designed by W.D. Caroe as early as 1903, but by 1909 only the main front and Library were ready for the official opening. The north wing was added in 1912 and completed in 1930, the south wing not until 1954, and the Park Place end of these wings as late as 1962. The original concept of a quadrangle closed in by a Great Hall was unfortunately abandoned.

University College of South Wales and Monmouthshire.

Secretaries of Clubs and Societies.

E. Owen   J. Evans   W. S. Hughes   G. H. Sutton   C. C. Blower   A. W. Jones   H. W. Hawker   I. Thomas
W. U. Williams
P. Bell   A. Jones   T. Matthews   M. Mordey   A. L. Embleton   T. T. Williams   G. Holding   R. T. Williams   F. W. Gibbon
G. Thomas   F. Whitaker   C. T. England   E. M. Jenkins   S. Auckland   E. Morgan   M. R. Hughes
H. Davies   A. James   G. Evans   G. Edwards

88. The University was very much the college of the people and form the outset recognised the place of women in higher education. The secretaries of College clubs and societies included a number of ladies in 1899, all very primly dressed with not a blue-stockinged ankle in sight. There was more variety of fashion among the men, from the public school cap on the left via an assortment of Dai caps to the bowler on the right; wing collars, turned-down collars, cravat, bow tie and one striped tie in the College colours of light blue and olive green.

89. In this informal picture George and Mary, as Prince and Princess of Wales, appear on the balcony over the main door of the College after the ceremony of opening the Drapers Library 1909. The undergraduates are in academic dress and white dresses beneath their gowns seem to have been *de rigeur* for the ladies, though there is a mixture of formality and informality among the men and boys looking on.

90. The Library in Old College, Newport Road, was severely functional, lighted by long windows and gas brackets with very heavy furniture on the bare boards. There is an air of solid learning about the large inkwells and massive tomes on the tables. Though women students are again in evidence, there seems to have been some voluntary segregation.

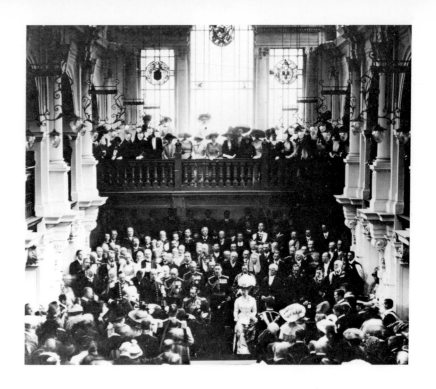

91. By contrast the Drapers Library in New College seems both luxurious and ornate. There is stained glass in the windows and the lighting is by electricity in elaborate wrought-iron chandeliers. Ladies in wide Edwardian hats throng the balcony for the speeches at the official opening in 1909. The crowd below is a catholic mixture of cultures and interests. Uniforms almost outnumber the academics and on the left the Bishop of Llandaff stands next to the Archdruid.

92. Education in Cardiff had come a long way from its humble beginnings in the charity schools. This scene inside Roath Village School in 1899 must have been typical of its day – the dame, cane in hand; the slates; the tall desks for the older children and a single form for the little ones; the pinafores and Eton collars; flowers for the teacher in the old ink bottle and vases on the mantle-piece; coal fire laid ready for lighting; and an attempt to brighten the dingy walls and convey sound precepts with an alphabet and picture of angels and Jesus the Good Shepherd. So, by our grandparents, was knowledge hardly won.

93. Thirty years later horizons were widening, and classes could visit Cardiff City Observatory for a lecture and demonstration by Mr. Dan Jones, F.R.A.S. The telescope had been built by George Calver in the 1870's for Archdeacon Conybeare Bruce at St. Nicholas, and was the largest in Cardiff until the University installed a new telescope on top of the Maths Tower in Cathays Park in the 1970's. The City Observatory and its telescope were the gift of Mr. Franklen Evans and were installed in 1925 at a height of 200 feet on Penylan Hill.

94. Howells School was founded at Llandaff in 1859 by the Drapers Company, administering the will of Thomas Howell, an Elizabethan merchant, whose bequest of dowries had been converted into an educational trust. By the time this photograph was taken in 1880 the name 'orphans' was being replaced by 'boarders', their dress was extremely elegant, and their surroundings and activities were very different from those of the village schoolchildren a few miles away in Roath.

95. The Victorian Gothic of Llandaff contrasted with the rather grim educational Edwardian of the city's secondary schools, established after the Education Act of 1902. But inside the schools were light and airy and educationists had accepted that children needed places to play and shelter from the weather in the sturdy playground sheds sadly lacking in modern schools. Some were even lucky enough to have their own playing fields but by the 1930's sport was not so elegant and gym slips and black stockings were compulsory wear.

96. In the elementary schools Welsh had become a class-room subject, though its teaching reflected the attitudes of a largely anglicised community. Since the mid-nineteenth century publishers of postcards for the tourist trade had been turning out 'Welsh' subjects – 'Oh! Those 'Welsh tea-parties'!' moaned a writer in *Folk Life* (1964). 'They are the most phoney of all the postcards... Alas, it became difficult for some people to visualize a Welshwoman unless she was sitting behind a teapot.' So, in 1930, Welsh culture is demonstrated in class by a genteel tea party in conventional national costume.

97. That costume was perpetuated in the mid-nineteenth century by the enthusiastic efforts of Lady Llanover, who encouraged the weaving and wearing of Welsh flannel and was largely responsible for the acceptance of an outdated fashion of the remote Welsh countryside as genuine national dress. Madame Hughes Thomas is seen here about 1900 with her Royal Welsh Ladies Choir who were to perform at many civic occasions, including the reception for Captain Scott. She dressed her singers in a charming Edwardian version of Welsh costume, with elaborate lace fichus and bonnet strings on their steeple hats. This is one of a set of postcards published by Glamorgan Archive Service.

98. Paradoxically, as the influx of population made Cardiff less Welsh in nationality, it became more consciously national, rivalling Swansea in its claim to be capital of Wales (not granted until 1955), and indulging in historical frolics like the National Pageant of 1909. During the fortnight of performances the part of Dame Wales was graciously performed by the Marchioness of Bute and Glamorgan (seen here) by her daughter-in-law, Lady Ninian Crichton-Stuart

99. C. Corn's 'Forget-me-Not Portrait Painting Company' of Cardiff published both these pictures as part of a set of sepia cards issued after the Pageant. A mock castle and miniature cromlech were erected in Sophia Gardens for the performances, given in the afternoons of the first week, the evenings of the second. Seat prices ranged from half a crown to 10/6 for the grandstand. The pageant began around A.D. 50 with Caradoc and culminated in the Act of Union of 1535.

The PASSING PROCESSION of PROMINENT PAGEANT PERSONAGES, as seen just now in the streets of Cardiff, free of charge.

100. A motley array of characters trooped the streets between performances and rehearsals and the *Echo* cartoonist has a field day in the comic picture postcard tradition with his 'Passing Procession of Prominent Pageant Personages as seen just now in the streets of Cardiff free of charge.' Note the hansom cab in the background and the knight in armour climbing the steps of the tram on the left.

101. Twenty-three years later a pageant on a similar scale raised £4,000 towards a new Students Union as a memorial to those from University College killed in the First World War. Support from the City was headed by the Lord Mayor, Alderman Hill-Snook, who exchanged his customary grey top-hat for a coronet to play Hugh Le Despenser, the Lord of Glamorgan who granted the most important of Cardiff's charters in 1340 — the culmination of this pageant. Music was provided by the National Orchestra of Wales. Historical authenticity was ensured by the professorial staff as writers, but civic pride overcame scansion in the 'Dramatic Prologue'

For we are citizens of no mean city —
In need of no man's patronage, nor pity.
Cardiff is past and present, and to come,
And of its glories we give but the sum!

102. For many years Cardiff had its own Orchestral Society, seen here at a performance in the Park Hall in 1901. Each year they gave three concerts during the winter season and held a triennial Music Festival in the same hall. Dr. Joseph Parry was their conductor from 1889 to 1892, Madame Patti performed as soloist in November 1890 and among their accompanists was Madame Clara Novello Davies, mother of Ivor Novello. She is seen here at the grand piano.

103. The audience, all of course in evening dress, was equally impressive. The programme that evening included the guest appearance of Dr. Frederic Cowen, who had made a special journey to Cardiff to conduct the orchestra in some of his own compositions. This flash-light photograph was taken during the interval by Messrs. Fradelle & Young, of London. The Park Hall later became a cinema and is now incorporated into the Park Hotel as the Theatre Suite.

104. All around the fringes of the growing city, woodland and open country were falling prey to the developer. Lovers Lane, Plasnewydd, pictured here by G.H. Wills in March 1882, was built over by 1890, as the suburb of Roath became a densely packed complex of streets. The 3rd Marquis of Bute was aware of the need to preserve a 'breathing space' for Cardiff's citizens, and in 1887 he gave the land for the first of Cardiff's public parks.

105. In this he followed the example of his mother, the widowed Lady Sophia, who in 1858 had opened to the public Castle Green (the parkland across the river now known as Sophia Gardens). In 1902 the Royal Agricultural Show was among the many annual cattle shows there that brought the country into the town.

Roath Park Lake, Cardiff.

106. The Corporation spent £62,000 on laying out the land given by the Marquis along the banks of the Nant Fawr, and Roath Park was opened to the public in 1894. This card bears the arms of the Borough and is unusual in that all the printing on the reverse is in Welsh as well as English. This Strand series was commissioned in Cardiff but printed in Bavaria.

107. This postcard, produced for J. Gulliford of 20 St. Mary Street, shows the landing stage on Roath Park Lane where rowing boats can still be hired and the swans fed as they were in this picture from the turn of the century. Houses are beginning to spread from a central block in Lake Road East.

108. Across Roath Lake, an Edwardian period piece is captured by the photographer who, unusually for a postcard, seems to have been more interested in the people than in the view. Boys are fishing in the lake but mother and daughters are so formally dressed that only a promenade is suitable.

Roath Park, The Bandstand, Cardiff.

109. In the lower section of Roath Park, the chief attraction was the bandstand. Large crowds came to hear the band play each Wednesday afternoon and evening from May to mid-September. This Raphael Tuck card in his 'Plate Marked Sepia' Series is postmarked 1911 and on the reverse is a description of 'this pretty park and pleasure ground presented to the people of Cardiff by the Marquis of Bute. It lies to the north of the town, and is easily reached by an omnibus from St. Mary's Street.'

110. The lighthouse-clocktower beside the boating lake is Cardiff's chief memorial to Captain Robert Falcon Scott and his companions who, in the words of the inscription *sailed in the S.S. Terra Nova from the port of Cardiff June 15th 1910... to locate the South Pole, and in the pursuit of that great and successful scientific task, laid down their lives in the Antarctic Regions. March 1912. 'BRITONS ALL, AND VERY GALLANT GENTLEMEN.'* A weather vane of the silhouette of the *Terra Nova* swings over the gay little lighthouse, a strangely incongruous reminder to the pleasure-makers of those tragic deaths among the Antarctic wastes.

111. This watercolour by Captain Richard Short from a private collection in Cardiff captures the excitement of the occasion so graphically described by the Norwegian ski-ing expert Tryggve Gran, who sailed with Scott: *Neither before or since in time of peace have I heard such an uproar as that which make the air tremble as* Terra Nova *glided out of the docks. People in their thousands yelled as if they had taken leave of their senses. Railway wagons were rolled over a line covered with dynamite detonators, and vessels in their hundreds completed the noise with whistles and sirens. At the last lock gates we were met by a little squadron of beflagged boats, and with this as escort we steamed out into the open sea.*

112. Cae Syr Dafydd (Sir David's Field) was the gift to the City of Mrs. Charles Thompson. The name has been transferred to a new housing development nearby, and the playing fields and gardens are now known as Thompson's Park. In this view the errand boys have paused to admire the fountain with its bronze statue of a boy, created by Goscombe John in 1899. There was consternation when it was stolen in 1971 and discovered headless, but it has now been restored with a fibreglass head modelled on the original.

113. Victoria Park, once part of Ely Common, was landscaped in 1897. The little girls with the perambulator are standing beside the lake which was the home of Billy the Seal. In reality a female, Billy was discovered in a box of fish delivered to a warehouse in Custom House Street in 1912. Billy's death in 1939 caused more grief to the children of Cardiff than did the threat of war. On one famous occasion, floods enabled Billy to leave the lake and board a tram car at the Victoria Park terminus.

114. St. Luke's Church, Canton, is pictured during the flood of 1st November 1927. Canton was one of the suburbs which expanded rapidly even before its inclusion in the city in 1875. At that time it was said to be the largest parish in England and Wales, and St. Luke's, consecrated in 1914, was one of the new parish churches created for the growing population. When this photograph was taken there was no building between the church hall and the junction of Lansdowne and Cowbridge Roads.

115. As we have seen, Cardiff has a long history of flooding, due to its position at the mouth of the three rivers, Ely, Taff and Rumney, and to the combination of high tides with heavy rain in the valleys to the north. The adults and schoolboys are gazing at flood waters in Roath on 3rd October, 1903. Are they waiting for the electric tram? And will it reach them through water deep enough to reflect the tram wires and the elegant poles that support them?

116. Roath was one of the ancient villages engulfed by the spread of Cardiff. As late as 1890 fields still surrounded Roath Village with its school (No. 92), church, and this grist mill, which was not demolished until 1897. In the background of this photograph by Reverend J.T. Wordsworth is the new St. Margaret's, designed by John Prichard and consecrated in 1870. Prichard turned the Bute vault into an elaborate mausoleum and the Marquis paid the whole cost of the building, though, as the *Western Mail* noted: 'The design also includes a central tower... but this is at present carried only a few feet above the ridge of the roof, the remaining portion not being included in the present contract.' It was added in the mid-1920's.

Llandaff Fields.

117. In the right background of this view across Llandaff Fields is the corn mill powered by a stream running from the weir beyond the Cathedral. It was demolished in 1930 to make way for Western Avenue but the adjoining house is now incorporated in the offices of the Welsh Joint Education Committee. Though the tree on the left has gone, another generation of children still play around the fountain given by Mrs. H.M. Thompson in 1900. Looking out from their house close by in 1930, her husband expressed what many still feel of the transition from Cardiff to Llandaff — 'We transfer ourselves to a surprisingly different world; we breathe in another atmosphere.'

118. 'Landaph, soe named of the River Taf running by,' wrote Rice Merrick in 1578 in his *Booke of Glamorganshire Antiquities,* 'is an ancient City... in it standeth one faire great Church, comonly called Eglwys Tilo, being the Cathedrall Church of that Dyoces. An old Castle standeth in it, sometimes the Pallace of the Bishopps thereof.' Despite destruction and neglect Llandaff still retains its Cathedral and the ruins of the Bishop's Castle. As in many places connected with the settlement of the Celtic saints, there are several old wells. This is in Cardiff Road outside the Old Registry House designed by John Prichard, but the water is now inaccessible through the blocking-up of the archway.

119. The Dairy Well is now covered with stone slabs in the grounds of the Cathedral School, the residence of the Victorian Bishops, and here in 1870 Bishop Ollivant discovered this late tenth century pillar cross. He erected it in his garden but in 1939 it was fixed next to the Bishop's throne in the Cathedral. After the bombing it was re-erected in the south presbytery aisle, almost the only evidence of the pre-Norman church in Llandaff to-day.

The Green Llandaff. 1885

120. 'Though the situation of Llandaff is beautiful... the houses of the poorer people, lying away from the traffic of the main road... have unusually little of that neatness and accommodation, which either cleanly retirement, or the more frequent intercourses of society, afford.' Benjamin Malkin, writing in 1804, might have been describing these old houses still occupied on the Green in 1885. But G.E. Halliday, writing in 1902 after they had been demolished, remembered them as 'quaint old cottages'.

121. Halliday published both these sketches in his 'Notes on Llandaff Parish' in *Archeologia Cambrensis* in 1902. In the early eighteenth century these almshouses were described as being divided into nine dwellings maintained by the overseers of the poor. They stood at the end of Heol y Pavin just off the Green and were tiled with stone.

The Green, Llandaff.

122. This colour card, postmarked 1904, shows on the left the houses that replaced the cottages in No. 120. The girls in the big hats then fashionable ever for little ones, are passing the cross restored in 1897 to commemorate Queen Victoria's Diamond Jubilee. Here in 1188 Giraldus Cambrensis heard Archbishop Baldwin of Canterbury preach the Crusade, 'the English standing on one side and the Welsh on the other'. The Red Lion Inn, later Tower House, on the right, was demolished in 1924.

Llandaff Green

123. Another colour card postmarked 1904 shows a horse and carriage outside the west wing of Tower House. The Green was for centuries the site of Llandaff Fair, first mentioned in the Norman *Liber Landavensis* as one of the privileges of 'St. Teilo and his successors for ever'. Browne Willis wrote in 1718 of the scandal of fairs here on Good Friday, and by the close of the nineteenth century they had, according to G.E. Halliday, degenerated into 'a scene of such licence that it was a disgrace to the countryside. The boxing or fighting booths were notorious, and their probably sequence was the recent finding of a skeleton buried a few inches below the grass on Llandaff Green.'

124. Around 1910 Llandaff High Street presented an unprepossessing appearance as gradual demolition of the old thatched cottages cleared the way for modern building. Behind the hoardings on the left is Llandaff National School, with its rose window designed by John Prichard, but now replaced by a supermarket. The horse bus plied between the Black Lion and Cardiff Castle. The rather dismal prospect is closed by the gateway of the Bishop's Castle and White House Cottage, both still standing.

125. The Cathedral dominates this aerial photograph of 1923 and near the bottom left hand corner can be seen the gardens and ruined gateway of the Bishop's Castle. Tower House still stands beside the cross, and above the Green is the ivy-covered façade of the Cathedral Choir School damaged by bombing in 1941. Next to it stands the Canonry (now Pen Dinas) and Iwan Christian's Victorian Deanery (now Llys Esgob, the seat of post-war Bishops of Llandaff).

126. The demolition of Tower House revealed the detached campanile in ruins, as it is said to have been left by the attack of Owain Glyndwr in 1401. Behind it rises the west front of the Cathedral distinguished by the contrasting fifteenth century Jasper Tower and the Prichard Spire, completed in 1867. Because the Cathedral is built on the low ground beside the river, its bulk is hidden from the Green. 'Llandaff,' wrote Peter Leech, 'is a village with a vast surprise almost completely tucked away.'

127. The greatest of Llandaff's three richly decorated Romanesque arches stands behind the high altar in this nineteenth-century view. Urban's arch is dwarfed by the soaring presbytery arch of John Prichard's Victorian Gothic restoration. Despite its height, the effect was one of Victorian gloom. The Cardiff Handbook of 1926 advised visitors that the Rossetti triptych behind the high altar 'is somewhat difficult to see... except when the light is good; the afternoon of a clear, bright day should be selected, if possible'. The roof and furniture of the nave were destroyed by a land-mine in 1941 but most of the arches survive to add to that 'elusive richness' of which Peter Leech wrote.

128. The Lady Chapel dates from the thirteenth century and was the first part of the old building to be restored by Wyatt and Prichard. In 1934, a year after this view was taken, the original mediaeval reredos was restored to position behind the altar, which here is plain and rather bare. There is no pulpit in the Lady Chapel to-day, and the niches in the reredos have been filled with those flowers whose Welsh names are associated with the Virgin Mary.

129. In this colour card postmarked 1904, the Lady Chapel is to the left, at the east end of the Cathedral. This view was changed in 1956 with the building of the Welch Regiment Memorial Chapel beside the Jasper Tower. There is a glimpse of the old Deanery (now Llys Esgob) above and to the right of the Jasper Tower.

130. On the south side of the Cathedral, the choir of 1870 is grouped at the foot of Dean Conybeare's cross. Before the establishment of a separate choir school, the choirboys were drawn from Llandaff village school. Among them, seated in the centre on the lowest step of the cross, was William Goscombe John.

131. A picture of the adult Goscombe John, now a knight of the realm and an established sculptor, is inset in this newspaper photograph of the War Memorial he designed for the Green at Llandaff. On either side of the central figure, a schoolboy and a youth in civilian clothes represent the boys of the Cathedral School and the men of Llandaff village-city who gave their lives in the First World War.

132. To the west of Llandaff 'city' the road divides, the right fork leading to Llandaff Bridge and Llandaff North (formerly Llandaff Yard), the left to Llantrisant. The toll house stood here until a little after this photograph was taken in 1884, and it was the limit of the daily walk taken by the 'orphans' and pay-boarders of Howell's School under the regime of its first Headmistress, the redoubtable Miss Baldwin.

133. 'Within the Parish of Landaph,' wrote Rice Merrick, 'are diverse Hamletts: Eley, Faire Water, Canton, Gabalva...' Of these, now all parishes in their own right, Fairwater to-day has a population of 20,000. Yet at the beginning of the century J. Kyrle Fletcher could describe it as 'one of those charming names which prepare you for a little sleepy hollow, where houses peep out from the rural beauties of well-trimmed hedges, and a little quiet stream flows down to the Ely River.' The atmosphere is captured in this view by William Booth in 1890, at the junction of Fairwater and Plasmawr Roads. Major David's house, in the background, became the Reardon Smith Nautical College and is now a Hall of Residence of the South Glamorgan Institute of Higher Education.

134. Swiss Cottage stood at the junction of Plasmawr Road and St. Fagans Road, then a country lane. Despite its flagged floors, mullioned windows and half-timbering, the cottage dated only from the 1890's, part of a nostalgic return to Tudor building styles illustrated by a row of similar houses in Cardiff Road, Llandaff. There was general regret when Swiss Cottage was demolished in 1972. The barley-sugarstick chimneys were carefully lifted off by crane and shipped to the United States.

135. Across the road, on the site of Fairwater Library and the council houses between Doyle Avenue and Fairwater Road, stood Brook Farm, pictured here in 1890 and demolished in the building boom which followed the Second World War. The Welsh name for Fairwater is *Twlch Coed* or *Twllgoed,* disguised in a sixteenth century English version in Leland's *Itinerary* as *'Tilthecoit* a pretty Village about half a mile from Lay (Ely) Bridge by the East Ripe (Bank). There is some meatly good Corn Ground in sum Places of this Commote of Landaff: and very good Frute for Orchardes at *Tilcoyth.'*

136. Some of the 'meatly good corn' is being cut in this oil painting by W.B. Witcomb of a farming scene typical of the area as late as 1930. These are now the playing fields of Waterhall School on a council housing estate of the 1960's and 1970's.

137. In less than a decade, farming in Fairwater had become mechanised, and Mr. Thorn had improvised his own 'tractor' in the field behind Brook Farm. The tall trees, a feature of the Waterhall Estate of the David family, still stand to-day in Fairwater Park and among the council houses.

138. Among his Fairwater studies in 1890, Booth photographed this youngster playing beside the cascade outside Brook Farm. Many people in Fairwater remember the little shed above the brook where in later years Mr. Thorn cooled his milk churns. The brook still flows alongside the road to join the River Ely. Everything else has changed.

139. Cardiff has always been a city of contrasts. Only a few miles from the little Fairwater fisherman, ragged children loll on the baking summer pavement in Helen Street, off Broadway, Roath. But childhood is resilient; the boy in the background has a hoop to bowl, the little girl on the right is holding the reins of the carthorse, and her older sisters play out the mazes of the games they have chalked on the paving stones.

140. The Romans may have come this way, and the Celtic monks making for the ford across the Taff. Certainly the Norman clerics travelled this road between their Bishop's Castle and his holdings in the village they called Bella Aqua. Roundhead soldiers marched to guard the crossings of the Ely. In the opposite direction generations of country folk travelled to Llandaff Fair and the children to Llandaff schools, as some of them do to-day. We began at the heart of Cardiff and have zig-zagged up and down the centuries and across the City. Let this old Fairwater road stand for all the travellers who through the years have contributed to the rich tapestry of Cardiff's history.